The Little Book of Puppets in Stories

Using puppets to enhance story telling
Written by
Simon MacDonald

Additional material and editing by Sally Featherstone

Illustrations by Martha Hardy

Little Books with **BIG** ideas®

The Little Book of Maths from Stories
ISBN 1 905019 33 5

© Featherstone Education Ltd, 2005
Text © Simon Macdonald, 2005
Series Editor, Sally Featherstone

First published in the UK, September 2005

'Little Books' is a trade mark of Featherstone Education Ltd

Published in the United Kingdom by
Featherstone Education Ltd
44 - 46 High Street
Husbands Bosworth
Leicestershire
LE17 6LP

Printed in the UK on paper produced in the European Union from managed, sustainable forests

Contents

The Little Book of Puppets in Stories

Introduction

"When children's own experiences connect in some way to those contained within a story, a match of meaning can occur. Such a match between that which children find important and the stories they read and hear makes the crucial difference between simply hearing a story and really listening with absorbed intent and making it part of their thinking."

Cathy Nutbrown - 'Threads of Thinking'

Using puppets to enhance storytelling sessions is not a new concept, but many practitioners have puppets which the are keen to use, but lack the confidence to use them

Using puppets is one way of encouraging children to talk about their experiences using the voice and actions of a puppet, a non threatening approach for children who may be less confident.

The use of puppets for story telling is a well known method across the world and for adults as well as children. Countries in every continent have long traditions of using puppets to bring stories to life - from Malaysia, Thailand and Indonesia in the East, through India, China and Russia, to France, Germany, Greece, Italy and Spain, there have been puppets for centuries. In the UK we have Punch and Judy on the beach, and they have crossed the Atlantic to join Pinnochio as icons for American children. Puppets have been described as 'being with us since socks were invented'!

And of course, modern puppets appear on TV shows as Kermit or Thunderbirds, they inhabit adverts and comics, and there are now even puppets with robotic features and superhero powers.

In recent years, the place of puppets in education has been recognised, and they are used with children of all ages to support storytelling and to explore sensitive issues.

Using puppets is one way of encouraging children to talk about their experiences using the voice and actions of a puppet, a non threatening approach for children who may be less confident.

The narrative and sequence of each story can be made clearer through them, allowing the child to slow down or catch up as appropriate. Puppets can also 'step out' of the story and make comment on the action or give hints as to what may happen next. Hopefully, you will be able to take the ideas contained within these pages and adapt them for your own use. This can open up a whole world of possibilities for your teaching and for children's enjoyment.

In this book we offer ideas for:

* using puppets to enhance the telling of traditional and familiar stories;
* making simple puppets that children will enjoy making and using in story sessions;
* making up your own stories with children;
* telling stories using a range of different puppets;
* helping children to use puppets to invent and imagine stories as well as retelling old favourites ad exploring their own experiences;
* exploring ideas, situations, problems and issues from home and at nursery or school;
* using bought puppets to encourage language development;
* working with small groups of children to make up their own characters and stories for puppets they have made themselves;
* using puppets to encourage thinking skills and problem solving.

Many practitioners will be familiar with the work Ros Bayley and Sharon Ginnis, practitioners and experienced advisers and writers on the use of puppets with young children. They are both practitioners who 'dare the children and adults they meet to just imagine...' We acknowledge their influence on our thinking and ideas for this book.

Links with the Early Learning Goals

Some of the stepping stones covered when working with puppets are listed here - you may identify others!

Personal, Social and Emotional Development
* show curiosity
* have a sense of belonging
* demonstrate flexibility and adapt their behaviour to different events, social situations and changes in routine
* show care and concern for others
* show confidence and ability to stand up for own rights
* have an awareness of boundaries set and behavioural expectations within the setting
* show willingness to tackle problems
* show a strong sense of self as a member of different communities

Communication, language and literacy
* listen to stories with increasing attention
* describe main story settings, events and principal characters.
* question why things happen, and give explanations
* extend vocabulary and use forms of speech influenced by experience of story
* consistently develop a simple story
* use talk to connect ideas, explain what is happening & anticipate what might happen next
* begin to make patterns in their experience through linking cause and effect sequencing, ordering and grouping

Mathematical development
* enjoy joining in with number rhymes, songs and stories
* show an interest in number problems
* observe and use positional language
* use size language such as 'big' and 'little'
* describe a simple journey from a story

Knowledge and Understanding of the World
* show curiosity and interest by facial expression, movement or sound
* show curiosity, observe and manipulate objects
* show an interest in how things work
* talk about what is seen and what is happening
* talk about significant events that they remember
* show interest in the world in which they live
* express feelings about significant personal events

Physical Development
* respond to rhythm, music and story by means of gesture and movement
* manage body to create intended movements
* manipulate materials and objects by picking up, releasing and arranging them
* use one-handed tools
* manipulate objects to achieve a planned effect

Creative Development
* work creatively on a small or large scale
* join in favourite songs
* use available resources to create props to support play
* enjoy stories based on themselves and people and places they know well
* introduce a story line or narrative into their play
* play cooperatively as part of a group to act out a narrative
* begin to use representation as a means of communication

Getting Started

Planning and preparation

We all have experience of puppets, whether through the traditional Punch and Judy show or the simple act of placing a sock on a hand and using a funny voice. Both are different but are not so far removed from each other. Puppets help to decentre children - they will sometimes confide in a sock more willingly than a parent! The use of puppets, whether home made or bought, is to be encouraged for many reasons.

* It is engaging - children cannot fail to be enchanted by such visits from weird and wonderful characters.

* It is child-centred - children, particularly very young children, are already holding conversations and sharing secrets and jokes with all manner of toys and puppets. By promoting their use in your setting or school, you are acknowledging children's current developmental stage.

* It is educational - puppets can be confronted about their behaviour, praised for their self-discipline, and asked for their advice in the space of just a few minutes. As role models, puppets are of great value.

* It is self-affirming - by showing the feelings and emotions, successes and failures of the children through puppets and soft toys, they are able to recognise experiences in their lives in a detached way, thus making the 'connections' that Cathy Nutbrown alludes to in the quote at the start of this book.

What follows is not just another book about making puppets, although we have included a number of types of these, along with appropriate activities. The book is designed to promote the use of story and song as well as to help practitioners to continue to explore the universal issues current in all settings - ways of sharing and behaving, valuing each other, giving space to acknowledge feelings of anger and sadness as well as happiness and contentment.

The Little Book of Puppets in Stories

Using Puppets in Story sessions

Helping you **to tell the story**:

Remember this does not need you to put on a funny voice and make a huge performance out of it. Many practitioners present puppets as a presence, holding it up to their ears to talk. In this simple but ingenious way, they give the puppet credence but don't have to have studied under great puppet masters for years!

Ros Bayley makes the point that:

'Many early years educators are natural storytellers, the only trouble being that not all of them realise that they are!'

Clinging to a book may give you some security, but it can restrict your contact with the children. We all know the story of Cinderella or The Enormous Pancake; we don't need a book to help us tell it. Putting down the book frees you to make eye contact with your audience, use a puppet and use gesture for expression. Relevant puppets can enhance the story further.

During the telling of any story, try pausing to allow the puppet to ask the audience what s/he should do. The puppet can then listen to the advice of the children and consider it before telling the group, through you, what s/he chooses to do. This values the children's responses as well as helping them to explore the feelings associated with the themes of the story.

The puppet can also can make appropriate responses - "I wish you had been there to help!" or "I would never have listened to that wolf if you had been with me!"

Puppets allow for questioning of motives and there is nothing more powerful than a group of young children grilling a wolf about his eating habits only for him to turn around and say that he doesn't like eating people and would prefer another menu! And of course, this idea could be used to explore healthy eating as a topic, and by the end your puppet wolf may have become a converted vegetarian!

Helping to support the story:

By providing the timing and the space for children to enact the story as you tell or read it, you are empowering them to perform with the structure and pace that you provide. It is not simply down to them, they are able to interpret the words and action of the story as it unfolds before them. As their confidence grows, children will begin to contribute their own ideas, nuances and twists to familiar stories, while you retain ultimate control. This is a way of familiarity can breed invention!

Reading the story:

Sometimes you can arrange for a puppet to 'read' the chosen text and rely on the children to help with difficult or unfamiliar words. Naturally these key words have been identified by you beforehand, but using a puppet to highlight these words, will make children more confident in making a contribution if they think that they are helping someone else! This is particularly valuable with smaller groups of less able or reticent talkers and readers as it serves as a confidence booster.

Telling creation stories:

There are many creation stories from different faiths and countries, and you will find that your telling these will be enhanced by the use of puppets. Try to collect some puppets from different beliefs and cultures to assist you in telling stories from other cultures and beliefs. Try asking parents and friends to look for these when they are on holiday (airport shops are often a good source!), or contact your multicultural service to see what they can offer. These puppets will provide your children with a new and rich experience as well as giving a authenticity to the story.

Using found materials:

Try using found materials to create puppets for use with these age-old stories. Cleaned and painted stones found on beaches have a lovely weight and texture, and a family of stones - beginning with the smallest right up to the largest - in a special purse or pouch can help you tell the story of how the mountains came to be. Interesting pieces of driftwood often have natural features that with a little sanding can be made into the most wonderful characters for use at storytime. These and other natural objects can help you to create entrancing stories for children.

Once upon a time....
Using traditional stories

There are now a huge number of manufacturers of large and small character puppets. Many of these are based on characters from traditional stories and rhymes and will be familiar to both practitioners and children alike. There are many ways you can use these puppets effectively. here are some ideas based on the story of Red Riding Hood. You could use similar ideas for other familiar tales.

What you need:
* A story book of Red Riding Hood or any other traditional tale
* Relevant puppets - for this example, a girl puppet (with a triangle of red fabric tied round her head) and a wolf puppet. You could add more for children to use, eg a grandmother or a woodcutter

Your preparation:

Here are some 'dos and don'ts for telling traditional stories with puppets:

don't try to learn the story by heart from a book. It will sound stilted and false, and you will be anxious.

do try to relax and enjoy it, if you forget what comes next, ask the puppet or the children, they will love to tell you.

don't get too anxious about getting a 'correct' version of the story. Children need to know that there are variations in stories, specially when they are told rather than read. They may tell you that their parents tell the story differently. This needs to be seen as a good thing. As long as the events happen in a predictable pattern, small variations make good talking points.

do tell different versions sometimes (perhaps one where Grandmother outwits the wolf). You need to warn the children, so they can spot the difference, or even give you a new or surprising event or twist to the tale.

don't feel you must use character voices.

do make a character for the puppet by telling the children about him/her/it - where they are from, what they like to eat, their name etc.

don't make the session too long, this will make you anxious.

do make the session short and enjoyable, then you will want to do it again. And plan some relevant songs and rhymes to start and finish the session.

don't abandon reading stories from books.

do enjoy stories in different ways - read from books, told with a book, told without a book, on tape, CD or video, in other languages, told by parents or grandparents.

don't restrict the puppets to story times

do use them throughout the day, indoors and outside, in every area of the curriculum. Make them characters in your setting, take them everywhere, sit them where they can see what is going on, invite them to group times. Then they will have plenty to say!

11

The Little Book of Puppets in Stories

Getting the setting right:

Make sure you provide enough space for children to act out parts of the story as you tell or read it. This will empower them to join in simple performances in the safety and order that you provide. They can interpret the words and action of the story as it unfolds, and act t out, either for their friends or as a group interpretation (everybody being the wolf etc).   As their confidence grows, they will begin to add their own nuances and twists to scenes, characters and movements, while you retain overall control. This way of internalising a story, scene or action and producing it through movement is a powerful learning tool for young children.

Some tips:

- ☺ Never force children to perform or join action, just gently encourage them; some children just want to watch;
- ☺ Give children a chance to discuss with a friend what might happen next, how a character might might behave or move, what a character might say or do;
- ☺ Use the puppet to lead the action, stopping and starting sections of the action or the story;
- ☺ Add some relevant finger puppets to your story session. This may tempt reluctant speakers or listeners to get involved.

Using the puppet to help with the story:

Puppets can help you in various ways; they can:

- 🖐 talk in your ear, making suggestions and asking questions;
- 🖐 tell bits of the story;
- 🖐 interrupt; making comments or butting in;
- 🖐 watch the children and choose volunteers for contributions;

- 🖐 become one of the characters, with or without a character voice;
- 🖐 tell the whole story, with or without a character voice.

Using found objects and giving them characters to help learning:

Don't forget that you can give characters to all sorts of objects, and these will help you to tell the story of real and fictitious events.

You could:

- 🌸 collect characters, animals, dolls, puppets and other objects when you are on holiday. These can bring stories and discussions to life in other areas of the curriculum;

- 🌸 use your imagination with found materials; such as a family of cleaned and painted pebbles of different sizes in their own special bag, unusually shaped pieces of driftwood; bark, cones, even big leaves can be torn or bent to make an interesting character, or an apple or potato with an interesting shape;

- 🌸 when you are introducing a new concept, think how you could incorporate materials and found objects; a fish toy can introduce a water topic, an African doll can help with Handa's Surprise, a stone can help to explain how rivers run and the rain cycle works;

- 🌸 bargain shops often sell cheap puppets and sets of characters; get them when you see than, and put them in your stock!

Be confident:

Remember, using a puppet to help you to tell a story from a book does not require a special voice or making a huge performance out of the activity. You could add a puppet as a presence, holding it up to your ear so you can listen to the comments. In this simple way, you can make the puppet a real character without being a puppeteer or using character voices.

Remember what Ros Bayley said (she is a renowned user of puppets in the early years) says 'Many early years educators are natural storytellers, the only trouble being that not all of them realise that they are!'

The Little Book of Puppets in Stories

Once upon a time....
The Jackal and the Rabbit

This story is one of Aesop's Fables. It's about an ungrateful jackal and how a clever rabbit tricks him when he doesn't keep his promise. It gives a wide range of opportunities for using puppets in different ways.

What you need:
* a soft toy rabbit
* a glove puppet jackal (a dog or other toothy animal will do)

The story (this story is about playing tricks on people who try to help you) :

A jackal was digging under a rock looking for something tasty to eat when the rock rolled over onto the jackal's paws and trapped him there. Try as he might the jackal could not get free.

He started to shout and before long a rabbit hopped into view. The jackal told the rabbit what had happened and asked if the rabbit would be kind enough to roll the rock off his paws.

'If you do, you will save my life and I'll be grateful to you for ever. I'll give you food and you can eat until you're full!' said the jackal.

The rabbit decided to help, and after a lot of panting and puffing, the rabbit managed to free the jackal. But instead of being very grateful, and preparing food for her, the jackal jumped at the rabbit and caught her in his paws.

'No! No! You dreadful creature!' shouted the rabbit, 'I've just saved your life and this is how you reward me!'

'I must,' said the jackal. 'I'm so hungry. If I don't eat you, I'll die!'

Just at that moment, an old man came by. The rabbit called out to him:

'Please, old man, please come here and help!' pleaded the rabbit.

The rabbit told the old man what had happened. When he had finished, the old man thought for a moment and then turned to the jackal and said:

'Jackal, you have been very naughty! You lied to rabbit. Let her go right now!'

The jackal was cross. He bared his teeth and growled.

'How dare you talk to me like that? I'll eat rabbit and then I'll eat you!'

The old man opened his eyes wide and pretended to look frightened. Then he played a trick on the jackal.

'Maybe if I saw what actually happened, I could get the right story. You say you were trapped under a rock?' said the old man. 'Where was this rock?'

The Little Book of Puppets in Stories

The jackal dropped the rabbit and ran over to the rock.

'Here! Here it is!' shouted the jackal.

The old man walked around the rock, shaking his head.

'And where were you when the rock rolled onto your paw?' asked the old man again.

'Here! Here!' said the jackal, a little impatiently this time.

'And 'But you are just a small and weak little animal. How did you manage to roll this great big rock off the jackal's paws?' said the old man.

'Like this!' shouted the rabbit,
and she pushed the rock until it rolled back <u>onto</u> the jackal's paws and trapped him once more.

'Ahh! I see!' said the old man. 'So this is how you found the jackal?' he said to the rabbit.
The jackal nodded too.

'Then that is exactly how you shall leave him too! Come rabbit and let us leave this ungrateful animal right where he is!' said the old man.

And that is what they did.

The moral of this story is about the importance of keeping promises when someone helps you.
The jackal is left to think about whether it was a kind thing to trick the helpful rabbit.

Ways In: There are a number of ways to illustrate this tale with the help of puppets.

Firstly - a straight telling, using the soft toy and puppet operated by the teacher/practitioner. The role of the old man can be offered to any member of the audience, and introduced like this...

'Just at that moment, Maeve came by...'

Everything that Maeve says is first said by you in your role as teller, so she doesn't have to produce any improvised dialogue. She will soon become deeply involved in the tale, and as she becomes more confident, will react and respond more naturally to the other characters and the events. The ending should allow for her to leave holding the rabbit and hold it until the session ends. This supports continuing empathy.

Secondly - you may wish to elaborate the ending by:

- asking for the help of another child to talk to the jackal about its behaviour
- allowing the puppet to be released and go and sit with another child as an alternative ending, emphasising the notion that behaviour is changeable just as our actions are.

Thirdly - the puppets can be hot seated. This is method allows for actions and events to be analysed outside the narrative, either at the end of the story, or at intervals during the story.

For instance, the jackal could be made to confront his behaviour or the rabbit could be encouraged to give the jackal another chance.

A child may be chosen to sit in the 'hot seat' with the puppet to act as its voice.

All the above ideas can be adapted to the wealth of stories and narrative rhymes available to you and your children. With a little more imagination, the stories can exist outside the pages of their books, and can consolidate the attitudes and dispositions you wish to encourage in your setting.

The Little Book of Puppets in Stories

Make it move!
Action songs and rhymes

This section looks at how you can easily include work with puppets in other areas of the curriculum. The section contains examples of Mathematical Development through the focus of Minibeasts and Knowledge & Understanding of the World through a focus on the weather.

What you need: for centipedes
* paper plates, ribbon or paper strips, felt pens
* a few garden canes or sticks

What you need: for snow people
* cotton wool, coloured dots for other puppets, provide
* card, felt pens, foil, polystyrene

Centipede and Millipede:

Centipede has lots of legs
To climb up garden walls;
They stop him from falling off,
He counts them as he crawls.

CHANT: Zero, ten, twenty, thirty, forty, fifty, sixty,
seventy, eighty, ninety, one hundred!

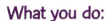

This lovely song introduces the concept of large
numbers to young children. They love to talk and
laugh about astronomical figures from a very early
age and we should not shy away from letting them
explore this. Once you have sung the song (to the
tune of Jack and Jill), you can work together to make a centipede puppet
with as many legs as you like!

What you do:

1. Each child decorates a paper plate (or a circle of stiff paper).
2. Get a volunteer to make their plate into a head for the centipede/
   millipede.
3. Now add strips of paper for legs (as many as you like)!
4. Tape or staple the circles together to form the body of the centipede.
5. Fix sticks at both ends of the creature, and at intervals along the body,
   so several children can work the puppet.
6. Sing the song while the children move the puppet so its legs and body
   wiggle.

and another idea:

Children could make individual centipedes and millipedes
from socks or tights stuffed with paper and segmented
by wrapping elastic bands round at regular intervals.
Add some eyes, and legs of wool, string or pipe cleaners.
You could also make caterpillar puppets to accompany
Eric Carle's story 'The Very Hungry Caterpillar'.

A Centipedes

Or you could use this very old poem:

> A centipede was happy quite, until a frog in fun
> Said, "Pray, which leg comes after which?"
> This raised her mind to such a pitch,
> She lay distracted in the ditch, considering how to run.

What you need: paper, plastic or polystyrene cups, string, wool or pipe cleaners, felt pens/paint/sticky shapes, glue/tape, card or paper to cover the open end of the cup

What you do:

* each child takes a cup and decorates it with pens, paint or stickers;
* help the children to cover the end of each cup with paper or card;
* then attach legs by cutting lengths of string or wool, laying the cup ion its side and draping the legs over the cup, securing them in the middle of the string with tape or glue;
* stick the cups together to form a long centipede (you decide how long!);
* add some eyes and feelers to the front cup;
* you can work this puppet either by tying strings on at regular intervals or letting children hold the centipede with their hands under its body. In either case, you will need several children to operate it.

and another idea:

* make a millipede with even more legs;
* find out the difference between centipedes and millipedes, where they live and what they eat;

* go on a minibeast hunt in your garden or the park; lift logs and stones and see what you can find.

Ten Little Snow friends (Helen McGregor; Tom Thumbs Musical Maths; A&C Black):

Puppets which reflect the weather conditions outside are easy to make and fun to use in any early years setting. You can explore what it is like to be a raindrop or a cloud, move a puppet like the wind, have a conversation between thunder and lightning.

What you need:
thin white card or paper to cut into strips, felt pens, scissors, glue or masking tape, cotton wool

What you do:
* you could use the cotton wool to wrap round each child's index finger, adding some dots for eyes;
* or you could just make white paper tubes to slot on fingers. Children could have one each, or even ten to use both hands.

The poem goes like this, there is no tune, just chant:

Five little snowmen going for a walk,
Five little snowmen stopped for a talk,
Along came five snow-women, then,
They all danced together and that made ten.

Ten little snowfriends danced all night,
Under the moon and stars so bright,
Early next morning up came the sun,
Warmed all the snowfriends, so then there were none!

In the first verse, children use one hand, showing the five puppets. Then along comes the other hand showing the other five. The second verse has the ten fingers wriggling about and then at the end, the fingers make fists as the snowfriends melt and disappear. As alternatives to finger puppets, try drawing smiley faces on each fingertip. Be creative and be flexible!

and another idea:
* make simple snow people shapes from card, cover with cotton wool and add a lolly stick for the operator to hold; now ten children can work together during the poem;
* make snow people finger puppets from the fingers of a glove. Cut each finger off and cover with cotton wool.

The Little Book of Puppets in Stories

How are you feeling?.
Using puppets to explore feelings

This section looks at how you can use puppets in stories that address difficult issues and feelings. The use of puppets is a great way to explore desirable and undesirable behaviour, relationships, new experiences and difficult situations. The example here involves the use of a soft toy, doll or puppet to help young children become problem solvers and thinkers.

What you need:

* A simple soft toy, doll or puppet (a teddy, soft dog, 'persona doll', boy or girl puppet etc) a new puppet will quickly acquire a personality!

* a small bag with personal belongings for the puppet
* a sensitive ear to pick up issues that may be troubling or interesting the children

Telling the story, exploring the problem:

Sit the puppet on your knee and introduce them to the children. Spend some time discussing their character, their name, where they live, their favourite activities etc. It's worth giving some time to this stage, so the children feel they have been joined by a real personality.

Show the children the puppet's bag and explain that s/he keeps special things in it. Now tell the children that the puppet is feeling particularly sad today. The reason is that they have lost something from their special bag.

Talk about precious things and ask the children what their precious things are. Discuss how we feel when we've lost something precious; ask the children if there is anything they can think of to say to their sad puppet friend that might make them feel better.

Now ask the children to suggest what might have happened to the lost object. Some suggestions might be:
* someone could have taken it;
* perhaps it fell out of the bag;
* perhaps the puppet put it down and forgot to put it back in the bag;
* perhaps it's somewhere in the room;
* it might be underneath something.
Encourage the children to make their suggestions to the puppet.

Talk about how the character feels about their loss and discuss what we should do if we find something that doesn't belong to us. Ask the character to give a detailed description of the missing item and where they remember last seeing it.

You may have already 'mislaid' the item for the purposes of this activity. Tasking the children to go off and search ensures that, as if by magic, the item is found and returned to a very relieved and grateful puppet.
Everyone is happy and the children are praised for helping and caring. Now the puppet can talk about their special item, explaining how they came by it and why it is so important to them.

The Little Book of Puppets in Stories

Developing questioning skills using "The Frog Princess":

You can also use puppets to develop questioning skills.

Try this:
- 🐸 Put a character (a soft toy, puppet or doll) in a bag or box;
- 🐸 Let the children ask you questions about who is in the box/bag. Younger children may need some clues.
- 🐸 When they have guessed the character, ask the children to suggest a name for it.
- 🐸 Now explore why a frog, for example, is living in a bag or box. This will involve finding out about what the children know about a frog's natural habitat.
- 🐸 Ask the frog if s/he would like to be shown around the new environment they now find themself in.
- 🐸 Two children at a time can take on this task, involving the frog in all the activities that the children experience for the rest of the day. Make time before the end of the session so the children can report back on the story of what they showed the frog.
- 🐸 This is a very good way of reinforcing what children have done and learned during the day. There is nothing like having to teach someone else for helping you to learn!

If you have enough puppets or soft toys, then each child in your setting could be given one to befriend for a day.
Some forward-thinking practitioners regularly send these toys home with children at weekends so the child can look after it and record their time together through photos and a diary which is then shared on their return after the weekend.

Sounds good....
Using puppets in phonic activities

The following activities use glove puppets to develop listening skills and consolidate learning in recognising initial sounds and developing alliterative knowledge.

Links with the Early Learning Goals

CLL   Distinguish one sound from another; show awareness of rhyme and alliteration; hear and say initial sound in words and know which letters represent some of the sounds.

What you need:
* different colours of felt, fur fabric and fabric scraps, pens, sticky dots
* glue or needle and thread

What you do:

1. Help the children to make some animal finger puppets from felt. Decorate them with scraps of fabric, felt pens etc. Add eyes, ears, tails etc. Younger children could make finger puppets from tubes of felt or fur fabric prepared earlier by you. The children could then add eyes and decorate them. Encourage all children to talk about what they are doing as they work.

2. When the children have made their puppets and decided which animal they will be, add the initial letter of the animal on the front of the puppet (use a marker or a cut out letter).

3. Now encourage the children to play freely with their puppets. Observe this play and note any reference the children make to the letters on the puppets.

4. Gather the children together and say you are going to play a sound game with all the puppets.

5. Ask each child to think of a name for their puppet that starts with the same letter as the one on their front:
   Tommy Tiger, Eddie the Elephant, Martha the Mouse etc
   Note the names so you don't forget!

6. Go round the group, each child introducing their puppet to the group - 'Hello, I'm Teddy Turtle'. Older children could work in pairs saying 'I'm Teddy Turtle, who are you?'

7. When all the children have introduced their puppet, make up some simple stories together involving the puppets -

'Martha Mouse, went into the forest where she met Tommy Tiger. He was stuck in the mucky mud, so Martha mouse had to pull him out.'

'Gerry Giraffe was munching on leaves at the top of the tree when Mike the Monkey jumped out from behind a leaf and made Gerry Giraffe jump.'

The Little Book of Puppets in Stories

Keep the stories short and simple, and as the children get used to the format, invite them to join in -

Clarrie the Cow walked down the lane. She met ???? and ???? and ???? they went to the pond for a drippy, droppy drink. Try to keep the alliteration going.

and another idea....

✳ As children get used to the idea of listening for sounds, you could use further sessions to ask other questions of individual puppets, such as:

Where does Lenny Lion live?	London
What does Lenny Lion wear?	leggings
What does Lenny Lion eat?	lemons
Who are his friends?	Lynn and Lorna

✳ Collect a treasure bag for each animal with things that start with the same sound.

✳ Make a zig-zag book from folded paper and draw something the puppet likes, does or has on each page.

✳ Make a picture story about one of the puppets, using digital photos and captions dictated by the children.

✳ Place different puppets around the setting, and give the children sound clues for finding them - Billy Bear is near something blue; Caspar the Cat is under something starting with c; Martin the Mole is in the ....; Simon the Seal is buried in the s.....

✳ Add the puppets to simple made up stories where they can be one among many characters. The two children met Penny the Pony who only liked things starting with 'p'; Down the road came Freda the Fox, who had found fifty feathers in the fountain; Digger the Dog ran down the street chased by three dustmen who all shouted 'STOP you've got our dirty dustbin lid!'

The Little Book of Puppets in Stories

and for older children....

* Introduce word endings - Meg only collects words that match her name and end in 'eg' (peg, leg, beg).

* or blends - Scrap collects words that start with 'scr', Spot collects 'sp' words, Shona collects 'sh' etc.

* or double letters Scooter the Seal collects 'oo' words, Fleet the race-horse collects 'ee' words.

Now try making stories with the word collections - 'Once upon a time, Meg had a sore leg. It was sore because she had tripped over a peg that was on the floor. Meg had to beg Sid to help her sit down...'

The Little Book of Puppets in Stories

Keep the beat....
Musical puppets

Puppet making can be extended to music, by making beaters with character and instruments with attitude.

Links with the Early Learning Goals

PD   Respond to rhythm, music and story by means of gesture and movement; manage body to create intended movements; manipulate materials and objects by picking up, releasing and arranging them; use one-handed tools; manipulate objects to achieve a planned effect;

PD   Work creatively on a small or large scale; join in favourite songs; sing a few simple, familiar songs; begin to build up a repertoire of songs; use available resources to create props to support play; introduce a story line or narrative into their play; play co-operatively as part of a group to act out a narrative; begin to use representation as a means of communication.

What you need:

* beaters and sticks, wooden spoons and spatulas
* paint, felt pens, sticky dots, ribbons, bits of fabric

Keeping the beat:

Work on beat competency (the ability to keep a steady beat) is now seen to be a key factor in future learning success. From an early stage, children need to practice clapping, stamping, playing simple musical instruments to accompany songs, rhymes and stories, as well as keeping the rhythm to recorded music.

Some ideas for accompaniments to steady beat work are:

- nursery rhymes
- number songs
- country dancing music
- brass band music
- percussion instrument playing
- clapping games

All these activities can involve puppets:

- as beaters
- keeping time held by an adult
- holding instruments such as drums
- encouraging less confident children to respond
- finger puppets on fingers for tapping and waving
- big puppets can hold beaters themselves and play the beat
- conducting the audience

Do it yourself....
Making your own puppets

The next section gives you some ideas for making your own simple puppets. Most of them can be made by children with minimum help from you, and many use recycled or economical materials. In this way you can provide simple puppet making as a free choice activity for children on a regular basis.

Spoon puppets

What you need:

* wooden spoons in different sizes (try bargain shops)
* felt pens, glue
* paint in flesh tones
* wool for hair
* fabric pieces
* elastic bands
* a mirror to check facial features

What you do:

1. Explain what you are going to do and invite each child to choose the size of spoon they want.
2. Look at the materials you have collected and talk about the sort of puppet they are going to make. You could:
   * let them have free choice;
   * link the puppets with a topic;
   * let them choose a character from a familiar story;
   * make a puppet of themselves or a friend.
3. help them to decide whether they want to use paint to match the skin tone with the character they are making. Use a mirror to check, if they need it.
4. Make some hair with lengths of wool or some fur fabric, and stick it on to the puppet's head.
5. Decide how to makes eyes, nose and mouth (with felt pens, sticky paper, fabric).
6. Help the children to make simple clothes for their puppet from squares or rectangles of fabric, wound round the spoon and secured with an elastic band. This fabric should be big enough to cover the child's hand when they are moving the puppet.
7. You could stick some cut out hands and feet on the edges of the clothing for extra effect.

The Little Book of Puppets in Stories

Using the puppets:

☺ Show the children how to hold the puppets under their 'cloaks', and when using them, to keep them facing the front or the audience.

☺ Now enjoy:
  * free play sessions
  * conversations between two puppets
  * using the puppets to accompany songs
  * making up stories with two or three characters
  * using the puppets in simple stories about the children themselves
  * using them to help with steady beat as the children tap or wave them
  * using them to ask questions and pose problems.

and another idea:

☺ Spoon puppets can also be used successfully in a simple theatres made from
  * a big cardboard box with a square cut from one side;
  * a curtain hung over a string tied between two convenient hooks (eg on a doorway);
  * a clothes airer with a drape over it;
  * a wall of big bricks;
  * or in the window of a home corner screen, or behind a chair.

☺ Leave materials and spoons for children to make their own puppets unaided as a child initiated activity. The children can use them in free play or in their own stories.

☺ Use a digital camera to take series of pictures of the puppets in stories and make simple books.

☺ Make spoon puppets for counting games and songs.

The Little Book of Puppets in Stories

Glove and sock puppets

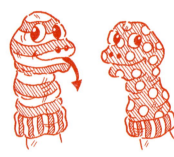

What you need:

* old gloves and socks (a great use for those odd items in the Lost Property Box or the Laundry Basket!)
* felt pens, glue
* wool for hair
* fabric and felt pieces

What you do:

Ask parents to donate odd socks to increase the variety!

1. Look at the different gloves and socks and play with them together to see what they can do. Try different sizes, colours and types.
2. If you poke the toe of a sock inside and hold it inside with your fingers and thumb, you can make the puppet talk.
3. Now talk about suitable characters for the puppets. Some ideas:
   * a brown sock for a dog, a bear or a horse;
   * a white sock with cotton wool fur for a lamb;
   * a black glove spider, with five legs and a body on the back of the hand;
   * a family of mice on one gloved hand, with whiskers, ears and noses.
4. Cut some felt or fabric for eyes, ears and tongues and help the children to stick them on. Cut lengths of wool for hair, or offer fur fabric. It's easier if the child works with their hand inside the sock or glove, leaving their other hand free to stick the features in the right places. They may need some help to do this!
5. Make some hair with lengths of wool or some fur fabric, and stick it on to the puppet's head.
6. Let the children decide on other additions - hats, scarves, decorations of sequins, beads, braid or lace bits.

Socks make great puppets with very expressive faces. Gloves are good for making group puppets - five mice on one hand, five little ducks, five members of one family. They are useful for counting songs and games, and give children practice in separating control of each finger (a pre-writing skill).

Using the puppets:

☺ Take time to talk about the individual puppets, naming them, talking about their characters, likes and dislikes and practising voices.

☺ Show the children how to hold the puppets and work them with their fingers, hands and wrists. Sock puppets work by moving your hand to make the mouth open and close, and moving your wrist to make them look at things or show emotions. Glove puppets need a bit more practice, but singing as they work them will help the children to control their fingers (as long as you don't sing too fast).

☺ Now enjoy:
* free play for individuals pairs and groups
* conversations and stories
* maths songs and rhymes
* to help with steady beat
* taking them outside often inspires children to become more involved
* or try letting the children take them home.

and another idea:

☺ Try conversations with a sock puppet on each hand.

☺ Make a simple puppet theatre by:
* fixing a piece of material on both sides of a door frame;
* cutting a window in a big cardboard box (from a fridge or washing machine;
* using your role play house window or a role play shop as a theatre.

The Little Book of Puppets in Stories

Plastic bag puppets

What you need:

* lots of small plastic sandwich bags
* sand
* elastic bands, sticky labels
* double sided or duct tape
* glue, permanent markers
* access to a laminator (if available)
* garden rubbish bags (green, silver, black, grey)

What you do:

1. Help the children to fill a small plastic bag each with sand till it is two thirds full.
2. Squeeze out all the air and fasten tightly with an elastic band
3. Turn the bag so the elastic band is underneath and pat the puppet into shape.
4. These puppets are more like 'beany dolls', and they make great puppet like toys to use in water or out of doors. Talk about the shapes the children could make:

* a fish	* a frog	* an octopus
* a whale	* a tortoise	* a spider
* a bat	* a bird	* a dragon

5. Discuss where legs, eyes, mouths, noses, fins etc. go and mark these with permanent markers.
6. Cut fins, eyes, ears, wings, legs etc from the coloured bin bags and stick with double sided tape or waterproof glue. You could use sticky labels or sticky backed plastic to make eyes and fins (or laminate paper shapes so they are waterproof).
7. Name the puppets, choose a voice and practice working the puppets, either by holding the top of the bag, or by taping a string or strings to the bag, the wings the legs etc.

The Little Book of Puppets in Stories

The natural habitats for these puppets are out of doors, in the sand or water tray, on the stones or grass, in the trees and bushes. Children will have a great time, simply playing or making up stories, creating environments and just having fun.

Using the puppets:

☺ This is such a simple activity that children can repeat it unaided. All the need is the offer of materials and adult help if they get stuck. They will enjoy the freedom and independence of making their own animals and people with different sized bags and different features. The simplicity of the method means that when the puppet gets waterlogged , torn or worn out, the children can easily make replacements

☺ As the children start to play with these puppets, talk with them about how they could make improvements to the movements. You could look at some video or pictures of the creatures, watching how they move and working to improve the ones the children have made. You could:
* attach strings to the wings of birds, bats and flying fish;
* tie thin elastic to spiders and butterflies to make them move;
* make fantastic creatures from stories with heads fixed on with pipe cleaners, claws made from plastic, spikes or scales on their backs.

☺ Read The Wide Mouthed Frog, The Rainbow Fish and other suitable stories to give children ideas for their own stories.

and another idea:

☺ Have an underwater puppet show in an aquarium. Make some very small plastic bag puppets and decorate them as fish. Add an octopus or two and even a shark made from a piece of grey plastic. Tie strings in the creatures and test to make sure they sink in water. Make seaweed by cutting strips of green plastic and tying small pebbles on the ends to keep them still under the water.
Then let the fun begin!

The Little Book of Puppets in Stories

Finger puppets

What you need:

* thin card or felt to cut into strips
* felt pens, scissors
* glue or masking tape
* wool for hair

What you do:

1. Cut some strips of felt, card or strong paper, long enough to wrap round a finger. Offer a range of colours to inspire different creatures or people.
2. Help the children to wrap a strip round their finger, and fasten with glue (or masking tape, which is easy to draw on). Remove the tube ready for decorating.
3. Talk about the different puppets they can make and get them to choose a character or animal before they start decorating the little tubes of fabric or paper.
4. They could use:
   * felt pens, paint, sequins, glitter or ribbon;
   * felt for ears, wool for tails, fur or cotton wool for hair or beards;
5. As they work, talk with the children about other features - does their puppet need ears? or wings? or legs? or feelers/ or whiskers?
6. Demonstrate how you can create great hairstyles, hats, feathers and crowns by fringing or curling small strips and shapes of paper.
7. Encourage the children to keep trying the puppets on so they can see their creation developing. They will also be able to begin to develop characters, voices .

These puppets are so easy to make, children will probably want to make more than one. They can also make them completely independently once they know how to do it.

Using the puppets:

☺ Children will often play independently with these simple puppets, retelling and making up stories of their own. Make sure they have somewhere quiet to do this.

☺ Other children may spend all day with the puppet on their finger, joining in the play, just being a companion.

☺ You can make simple finger puppet play part of your day by:

  * choosing relevant stories and asking individuals to contribute their puppet characters;

  * reading a story, then suggesting that children could make puppets to re-tell the story (The Three Bears, The Enormous Pancake etc);

  * selecting familiar songs which can be accompanied by finger puppet work;

  * Making up stories together, using the suggestions made by children and the characters of their puppets;

  * inviting children to tell their own stories, using their puppets as characters.

and another idea:

☺ Cut a box to make a three sided screen for a puppet show. Cut a window and put somewhere for the children to use informally with their finger puppets. They will come and say when or if they are ready for an audience for their plays!

☺ Use finger puppets for counting and number games. Get the children to make five puppets each (add a simple face and a number to each before putting them on. Play small group games where they have to show the right number in answer to your question or hold up number four/three/five when you ask.

The Little Book of Puppets in Stories

Make a giant snake

What you need:

* a long narrow piece of fabric (about 50-75cm wide and as long as you can make it)
* felt pens, PVA glue, paint
* wool, fabric pieces, bits of plastic, sequins, ribbon etc.
* old newspapers

What you do:

Any sort of fabric will do - a sheet, a curtain, a sari, even a shower curtain - knitted fabric doesn't fray so much. You could cut a wide piece in half and stick the ends together with PVA glue.

1. Explain that you are going to make a huge snake puppet and everyone can help.
2. Put the long piece of fabric on the ground (outside is best!) and let everyone help to paint it with patterns, spots, circle, stripes, zigzags etc. The more colourful it is, the better. Wait till point 6 before adding sequins and other decorations. You could:
3. When the paint is dry, fold the fabric in half and stick the edges and one end together with PVA glue.
4. Now get the children to screw up sheets of newspaper and stuff them in the snake until it is full (it doesn't need to be pressed down, just stuffed enough to give it some shape).
5. Cut the end of the tube so it makes a rounded end when you stick the final edges together.
6. Now you can decorate the snake with glitter, sequins, feathers or anything else you fancy, and decide how to make eyes, mouth, tongue etc.
7. Choose a name for your snake and then start to learn how to move it - this is an exercise in co-operation! It may take some time to learn, specially with younger children, but it is hugely enjoyable.

Using the puppets:

☺ The children line up beside the snake and each take hold of a handful of fabric from the top of the puppet.

☺ Now:
  * try taking the snake for a walk round the room;
  * invite your snake to join you for story and group times;
  * make the puppet dance;
  * make it undulate by lifting it up like a Mexican Wave;
  * take the snake up and down the slide, in and out of the home corner, all round your setting or school;
  * tell a story about the snake as the children (or some of them) act it out. Make the story simple and give the group of children time to move in a concerted way.

and another idea:

☺ Look for pictures of snakes, so you can add to the snake's patterns.

☺ Make smaller snakes using the same method, so children can play together.

☺ Use a digital camera to take pictures of the snake in action. Make a Snake story book of your snake in different places, doing different things.

☺ Do a snake dance, with some children leading the snake playing simple musical instruments.

The Little Book of Puppets in Stories

Ready to wear!
Using bought puppets

There are hundreds of different sorts of puppets on the market. No educational catalogue, exhibition or early years conference would be complete without a puppet stand. The final section of this book contains suggestions for using commerially produced puppets in your story telling sessions.

Pet puppets

People puppets

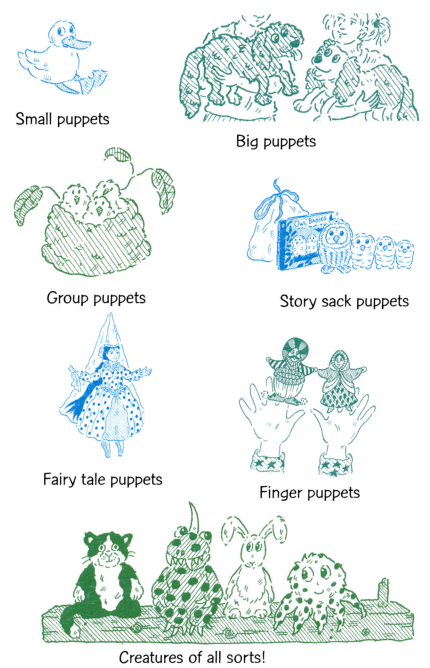

Small puppets

Big puppets

Group puppets

Story sack puppets

Fairy tale puppets

Finger puppets

Creatures of all sorts!

and many, many more...

The Little Book of Puppets in Stories

Story Sacks and Bags

What you need:

* one of the child sized commercially produced puppets - any character
* some props for your story, preferably in a bag: simple objects linked to your purpose for the session, a book, a pair of glasses, a camera, a piece of jewellery, a toy, a photo

What you do:

1. Remember that you don't have to make a special voice for the puppet, it doesn't even have to speak, it can whisper in your ear and you can repeat the words.

2. Introduce the puppet if the children haven't met it before. Give it a name and let the children ask it questions about characteristics, likes and dislikes. If you have another adult available, get them to note what you say so you don't make mistakes later!

3. Now introduce:
   * an incident staring the puppet 'Do you know, when Rory was little..';
   * a problem to solve 'Rory is very sad about ...';
   * a mystery 'Rory has lost...';
   * an invitation 'Rory wants to sing, play, find out about...';
   * a story 'Once upon a time, Rory...'.

4. Give plenty of opportunities for the children to contribute by offering chances to contribute:
   * their own thoughts, opinions and experiences;
   * how they think problems could be solved, feelings improved, behaviour changed;
   * where to look for a lost item, solve a mystery;
   * by joining in with songs and rhymes'.
   * by suggesting what happens next.

Using the puppets:

☺   Puppets can be used everywhere - outside, on a trip or visit, in the home corner or other role play area.

☺   You can use them to explore:
* **feelings**
* **relationships**
* **difficult situations** such as behaviour or worries; moving to a new class, nightmares
* **topics of current interest** by involving the puppets in discussion of music, current events, news
* **children's own knowledge of a topic** by telling the puppet what they know
* **descriptions** of unfamiliar objects and events

and another idea:

☺   Try:
* two big puppets having a discussion or dispute;
* using puppets to explore healthy eating and food;
* hiding one in the garden for the children to find;
* putting a puppet in the role play bed and talking about being unwell;
* get a puppet to ask the difficult questions when a visitor such as the dentist or nurse visits.

☺   Use big puppets with other toys - dolls, smaller puppets, soft toys .

☺   Take photos of your puppets in different situations and use them as prompts for stories and discussions. You could take a series of pictures and make a book.

☺   Hide or leave objects in your setting for the children to find and bring to discussion sessions.

45

The Little Book of Puppets in Stories

Making up a story starting with a puppet

What you need:

* a hand puppet - either bought or made yourself
* a collection of small objects (see below)

What you do:

1. The object of this activity is to involve the children as much as possible in the telling of the story. Don't be over-prepared, or you may not let the children have their say!.

2. Collect some small objects in a basket or drawstring bag, these should be scaled to the puppet you are using and could include:
   * a tiny notebook
   * a jewel, a bracelet or a little necklace
   * a pair of tiny glasses (from a Teddy Bear shop)
   * an empty perfume bottle filled with coloured water
   * a tiny teddy, doll or toy animal
   * a bag, box, or other container
   * a (magic) stone, pebble, bead or shell

3. Get into the habit of telling these stories often, and helping the children to understand that:
   * the same character can be involved in different stories on different occasions, even with a different name, home, characteristics etc;
   * every child's suggestion is valuable, but sometimes you have to choose one idea for today's story;
   * a story can be told in many different versions;
   * a story can go on over several sessions if desired;
   * elements of other familiar stories can be incorporated.

Using the puppets:

- ☺ Sit with the children in a comfortable, quiet area, children can sit in friendship or other partnered pairs, so they can talk about what might happen next, what the puppet should do, why something should be done etc.

- ☺ Remind the children that:
  - * this story has never been told before, and no-one really knows what is going to happen;
  - * sometimes you will choose one child's suggestion, sometimes another, children should be prepared to accept this. Working in pairs usually helps this!
  - * any idea can be considered;
  - * the story can be a repeat of one told previously, with little changes;
  - * the ending may be unexpected;
  - * you may make suggestions or add ideas.

- ☺ Introduce the puppet and start the story "Once upon a time ..." stopping for suggestions as you go.

- ☺ Don't forget to stop frequently to ask for suggestions, and give time for a bit of discussion with a friend;

- ☺ if the pace lags, use one of the objects in your bag -"Just then he saw a shiny stone/bottle/pair of glasses. What do you think ...?"

and another idea:

- ☺ Encourage children to offer their own found objects for stories.

- ☺ Leave puppets and objects so children can make up their own stories independently.

- ☺ Try leaving a puppet and a bag with one object for children to find and tell, draw or write the story.

- ☺ Start a story with the object, then introduce the puppet character later.

- ☺ Use this idea to make sequels to traditional and well known tales.

The Little Book of Puppets in Stories

Children as story tellers

What you need:

* a selection, box or basket of different puppets
* a quiet place
* some children respond better in one-to one or small groups for this activity

What you do:

1. Start with a simple approach:
   * just put one puppet and an object in the basket:
   * leave two puppets for stories involving two children;
   * choose a puppet linked to a story you have recently shred or a favourite of the children;
   * start with finger puppets, which are easier to use.
2. Tell the children that story telling with the puppet(s) is one of the activities they can choose.
3. Leave them to it, but if they are obviously finding it difficult to start try sitting in the area yourself to see if that gets things started.
4. Encourage children to retell their stories at plenary or group times, praising their independence and helping them if they find it difficult to remember what they said.
5. Encourage children to use puppets in your story times, always have some handy, so children bring them to group times, even just to sit with them.
6. Offer puppets as 'take home' activities instead of books - they stimulate a different sort of language activity. You could offer small sets of finger puppets for family play or even offer a big puppet to come on a visit home with a diary or disposable camera to record their stay. This could replace the more familiar soft toy and diary combination.

Using the puppets:

☺ Try offering finger puppets to any child who wants to take part in a free story telling session (see previous activity). You can easily incorporate them into a made up story by asking for a volunteer character to help, to suggest, to solve problems.

☺ Some more ideas:
  * put finger puppets in a 'feely bag' and let children pull out one to use in a group story;
  * bring a basket of similar small puppets to a story telling session - all woodland animals, all sea creatures, members of a family, characters form a fairy story;
  * let the children make finger puppets of themselves, and use them to explore things that have happened or make up stories about themselves;
  * they could make a puppet of an adult they know and use these to develop character voices and stories;
  * offer materials and opportunities for children to make their own little props for home made or purchased puppets.

and another idea:

☺ Make simple theatres together for the children to use from:
  * a big cardboard box;
  * a pop-up tent;
  * a drape;
  * some big bricks;
  * under a table.

☺ Take digital photos of the children using the puppets to add to their development files and as evidence of independent thinking, imaginative language, and problem solving.

☺ Remember that less confident children will often talk as a puppet when they are very reluctant to speak alone.

The Little Book of Puppets in Stories

Using a group of finger puppets

What you need:

* a collection of finger or hand puppets, all of a group or a random selection
* a quiet place to sit and talk

What you do:

1. It's a good idea to introduce this activity to small group, then you will be able to talk with each child about their puppet's role in the story. There will also be more opportunity for each child to contribute their ideas. When they have had some practice in small groups, it is quite possible to make a story with a whole class of children (specially the older ones) as long as you have enough finger puppets!

2. Put the puppets in a basket and explain to the children that you are going to make up a story together using the puppets.

3. Offer the basket to the children so they can choose a puppet each. You can have a puppet or not, as you wish. There are advantages to both!

4. Let each child think about their puppet and talk to each other about them, deciding on names, characteristics etc.

5. Now let each child introduce their puppet to the group, naming it and saying what it can do. You could ask older children to name a particular feature of their puppet - how brave they are, where they live, a magic trick they can do, a special gift they have etc. If children are hesitant or younger, you could introduce a puppet first to model what to say.

6. When this part of the activity is over, you are ready to start a story with the characters you have created together. You could offer the start to a volunteer, or start the story yourself .

The Little Book of Puppets in Stories

Starting a story:

☺ Some ideas for string stories with groups of puppets:
  * 'Once there were some friends ...'
  * 'In a little wood far, far away, there lived a ...'
  * 'One day a strange thing happened ...'
  * 'I was walking down the road one night when I heard a strange sound ...'
  * 'On a snowy day in a little house ...'
  * 'On the ground, small and round, a rabbit found ...'
  * 'The wizard who lived in the purple cottage had lost his glasses and needed some help to find them ...'
  * 'In a cave on a mountain, something wonderful happened ...'
  * 'Down by the river on a great big stone ...'
  * 'The bus was going to ...'

☺ Continue the story, stopping frequently for ideas from the children. As soon as you can, try to involve the puppet characters. You can:
  * use one as a main character;
  * involve a puppet as a player alongside the major character;
  * pose a problem such as finding something and ask who can help;
  * ask what happens next and give children time to discuss, predict and suggest;
  * get individuals to 'say' words through their puppet;
  * say 'What this needs is someone who...' or 'He needed to collect things starting with S'.

☺ The more frequently you stop, the more exciting the session will be and the more complex the story will become. You need to listen hard so you don't forget what the children have suggested - they are sure to remember!

☺ Use a camera to photograph individual children and their puppets. Then you can get them to dictate a caption about the character and the story.

☺ Later, the group could tell the story to other children.

The Little Book of Puppets in Stories

Using large animal puppets

What you need:

* puppets come in all sizes, and some are almost real life size. Among the most realistic are animals - dogs, monkeys, bears etc
* a bit of imagination!

What you do:

1. These large puppets are harder to manage than the smaller ones, and they take a bit of practice. You may want to have a go on your own before working with the children.
2. To introduce the puppet, you could:
   * bring it into the group in the morning, as if from home;
   * leave it in a basket or on a chair with a label round its neck;
   * pack it in a box and unpack it together;
   * get it delivered!
3. Discuss the puppet together, decide whee it came from, what its name is, what it likes and dislikes, where it lives/sleeps, what it eats, who it belongs to.
4. Remember that you don't have to make a voice for the puppet. It can answer the children by:
   * wagging its tail;
   * twitching its ears;
   * nodding or shaking its head;
   * whispering in your ear;
   * putting its paw on, or holding up cards or simple signs saying 'yes' or 'no'. Make signs with cards on small sticks to make them easier for the puppet to hold.
   * pointing to the child of their choice.

Don't forget to jot down some of this information in case you forget what was decided! You could make a passport or book about the puppet.

The Little Book of Puppets in Stories

Using the puppets:

☺ Once your animal puppet has a name and a character you can join their adventures. These can be:
  * made up by you;
  * made up by the children with your help;

☺ The puppet can also be used to explore current issues or problems (relationships, behaviour, breakages, loneliness, family difficulties), for instance
  * Stanley was in the park yesterday and he saw someone throwing stones at a bird. He was very upset. What do you think he could do if he sees it happen again?
  * Dora the dog is very happy about her new baby sister. She loves him very much, but sometimes she is sad because her mum is always with the baby and she's too busy to play with Dora.
  * Nellie the elephant is very sad because no-one will play with her. How can we help?
  * Yesterday, Greg the Gorilla found one of the books on the floor. It was all dirty and two pages were screwed up, and one was scribbled on! How can we make sure our books are all put back properly?

and another idea:

☺ Big puppets can also be taken home by the children for a night, so they can try them out in the security of their own family.

☺ Make beds, chairs, houses and props for your puppet.

☺ Take photos of the puppet in use and at rest in different places. Make a diary of their adventures.

☺ Get two big puppets to talk to each other, using both yourself, with two children in control or sharing the conversation with a child (or another adult!).

The Little Book of Puppets in Stories

Puppets, stories and sounds

What you need:

* puppets of any size
* simple sound makers or musical instruments eg:
  - sticks
  - shakers
  - rattles
  - rain sticks

What you do:

1. You could make some simple musical instruments with the children and then use them with the puppets in a puppet band. This means you can make lighter, smaller instruments which will be easier for the children to hold with a puppet. Here are some ideas:

2. Look at the materials you have collected and talk about the sort of puppet they are going to make. You could:

   * thread buttons, beads or little bells on strings so they rattle;
   * poke a short stick through the bottom of a yogurt pot or plastic cup, then thread a bead on the end of a piece of cotton and tape the cotton to the edge of the pot or cup. Shaking or twisting the stick will make the bead rattle on the cup;
   * saw broom handles into short lengths and decorate with paint or felt pen to use in pairs or by two puppets;
   * put a few grains of sand, some gravel or a few dried peas in one empty yogurt pot, cover with greaseproof paper fasten with an elastic band and use as a shaker;
   * stick sandpaper on small empty boxes or bricks to make 'scrapers', or saw grooves in a stick to make a guiros to scrape another stick along;
   * use small containers such as film canisters, plastic pots, little tins to make shakers. Attach to the puppets with strings or elastic bands.
   * stretch cling film over plastic pots and cups to make drums, and use lolly sticks as beaters.

Using the puppets:

☺ The children need plenty of practice in using instruments and puppets together, but it's a great way of developing hand and wrist muscles for fine motor control.

☺ Let the children have plenty of free access to different puppets and different instruments before using them in a more organised way.

☺ When you feel it is time, let the children (or those who want to) bring a puppet and an instrument to a story session. Start by telling very simple stories or rhymes and using the puppets to accompany characters, parts of the story or just the rhythm of songs and rhymes.

☺ Later, you can use the puppets and instruments to accompany all sorts of stories, from books, from your imagination, from real life or from the children's experiences.

and another idea:

☺ Encourage children to make up their own stories with sounds, or even sound stories with no words.

☺ Choose a few instruments, play them in a sequence, then make up a story to match.

☺ Take a tape recorder outside, round your setting or on a walk, record some sounds and make up as tory with the puppets when your return.

☺ Look for some small commercially produced instruments for your puppets to use:

* plastic 'egg' shakers
* mini maracas
* mini rainsticks
* small jingle sticks
* bell clips to clip on puppets' hands
* table bells with handles

(Suppliers in the resources section at the end of the book.)

The Little Book of Puppets in Stories

Puppets count!

What you need:
* five duckling finger puppets
* a Mother duck
  You can buy these as a set, collect them separately, or make your own with the children

What you do:

1. Puppets are great for counting songs and games. This one has a song/chant too

   'Five little ducks went swimming one day,
   Over the hills and far away,
   Mother duck said "Quack, quack, quack, quack",
   But only four little ducks came swimming back.

   Four little ducks etc.

   (when there are no ducks coming back, add this last verse)

   'No little ducks were swimming one day,
   Over the hills and far away,
   Mother duck said "Quack, quack, quack, quack",
   And <u>five</u> little ducks came swimming back.'

2. Five children have a duckling puppet each, another (or you) has the mother duck.

3. Talk about the puppets before you start, explaining how the poem goes.

and another idea:

☺ Let the ducklings come back one at a time (good for one more; one less practice).

☺ Say the rhyme substituting ducks with worms. Make eyes on each child's fingers with felt pen, and use them as worms. 'Five little worms went wriggling one day, off through the ground and far away.'

More counting stories:

☺ Make or buy **two** of each puppet and sing or say:
* Two Little Dickie Birds

☺ Make or buy **five** of each puppet and sing or say:
* Five Little Speckled Frogs
* One, two, three, four, five, Once I caught a fish alive
* Five Fat Peas

☺ Make or buy **ten** of each puppet and sing or say:
* Ten in the Bed
* Ten Little Men in a Flying Saucer
* Ten Little Leaves went Spinning Away
* Ten Green Bottles
* Ten Men Went to Mow
* Ten Fat Sausages Sizzling in a Pan

and another idea:

☺ Use puppets as you sing:
* Daddy's Taking us to the Zoo Tomorrow
* There was a Princess Long Ago
* Old MacDonald had a Farm
* I Went to Visit a Farm One Day

57

And finally; The Princess and the Wizard, a story starter for you to use with a group of children

What you need:

* this story uses two puppets, a princess and a wizard, but you could substitute them with any two story puppets and use the same outline
* a variety of animal finger puppets for the children

What you do:

This idea has been used with many groups of adults and children, it always comes out different, but it's always a really good story, and lots of people can be involved.

Make sure the children are comfortable and can see the puppets. They could also sit with a friend so they can discuss ideas for the story. Now let each child choose an animal finger puppet, give it a name and (with older children) decide where it lives and what it does. When children have had some practice at this, they could also give their puppet a special ability or a magic trick.

Let the children introduce their puppets to their friend or to the whole group. Ask them to be ready to help in the story, both with ideas and with their puppet characters. Then ask them to keep their puppets still until they need them for the story.

Before you start, it's probably best to agree some ground rules! These could include:

* everyone's ideas are valuable;
* if your idea isn't used this time, be patient, you will try to give everyone a turn;
* the puppets can be called different names, live in different places and have different adventures in different stories.

The asterisks (*****) indicate gaps for you to ask the children for ideas.

Once upon a time there was a princess, her name was (*****). She lived in a castle, where the roof was (*****), the windows were (*****), and the door was (*****). To get in the door you have to (*****).

Princess (*****) loved the colour (*****). She had (*****) curtains at the castle windows, (*****) covers on her settee, (*****) flowers in her garden. She only wore (*****) clothes and she only ate (*****) food, so her breakfast was (***** *foods of the colour*).

Princess (*****) climbed up to the top of the highest turret in her castle, round and round the twisty stairs, holding the rail made of (*****) so she didn't fall off the steps. When she got to the top, she was in a room with three windows. When she looked out of the first window she could see (*****). Which animals lived there?
When she looked out of the next window she could see (*****). Which animals lived there? *(children decide and hold up their finger puppets)*
Continue till she has looked out of all the windows.

As Princess (*****) looked out of the middle window, she saw her friend the wizard coming along the path. She saw him getting bigger and bigger, and when she could see his face, she could see he was crying! She ran down the stairs and opened the big wooden door of the castle.

"Whatever is the matter?" she said. "Oh dear" said Wizard (*****). I'm so sad because I've lost my (*****). Can you help me find it?"

"Of course" says Princess (*****) "I'll help you and so will all my animal friends." She went outside the door, took her magic (*****) from her pocket and when she (*****) it, all the animals came out of the forest. First came the ones who could (*****), then the ones who could (*****), then the ones who could (*****) *etc*.

When all the animals were gathered in the castle garden, among the (*****) flowers, the princess said "My friend (*****) the wizard has lost his (*****), who can help him to find it?"

The Little Book of Puppets in Stories

The animals were quiet for a minute, then one of them, the (∗∗∗∗∗) said, "I can help because I can (∗∗∗∗∗)."

"We can do that too, we will go and look in the (∗∗∗∗∗) for your (∗∗∗∗∗).

Continue with other groups of animals that can fly, swim, climb, dig etc.

All the animals hurried away to try to find Wizard (∗∗∗∗∗)'s (∗∗∗∗∗). And while they were gone, the princess and the wizard sat in the garden of the castle and ate some of the princess's (∗∗∗∗∗) food. They had (∗∗∗∗∗) and (∗∗∗∗∗) and (∗∗∗∗∗). The wizard was feeling much better, when they heard a sound. It was the sound of (∗∗∗∗∗), and they knew what that sound was. It was the horrible (∗∗∗∗∗). The horrible (∗∗∗∗∗) said in its horrible voice, "At last I have found you, Princess (∗∗∗∗∗). I know that the wizard is sad because he has lost his (∗∗∗∗∗) and so he has lost his powers and I can capture you and take you to my (∗∗∗∗∗). 'Oh no!" said the wizard as the horrible (∗∗∗∗∗) grabbed the princess and took her away.

What could the wizard do? (ask the children for ideas and pick one). The wizard tried (∗∗∗∗∗), but it didn't work. He ran to the castle gate and sitting on the ground just outside was a (∗∗∗∗∗) with a (∗∗∗∗∗) in its mouth. "I've found it!" said the (∗∗∗∗∗), it was (∗∗∗∗∗).

The wizard took the (∗∗∗∗∗), held it up and it (∗∗∗∗∗ed). A big (∗∗∗∗∗) came out and followed the horrible (∗∗∗∗∗) all the way to its cave. All the animals hopped and jumped and flew behind till they all cane to the cave. When the horrible (∗∗∗∗∗) saw the wizard's (∗∗∗∗∗) it screamed and (∗∗∗∗∗) . The animals carried the princess back to her castle.

She thanked the (∗∗∗∗∗) for finding the wizard's (∗∗∗∗∗) and she thanked all the other animals for being her friends. They all had a party with (∗∗∗∗∗) and (∗∗∗∗∗) and (∗∗∗∗∗), and (∗∗∗∗∗) to drink. Then they all played (∗∗∗∗∗) and (∗∗∗∗∗) till they were so tired that they all went home to bed.

The wizard and the princess went into the castle, climbed up to the room at the top of the tower and sat down. The wizard put his magic (∗∗∗∗∗) in its special (∗∗∗∗∗) and said "I'm so glad we rescued you, you are my very best friend." The princess said "Thank you, you are my best friend too."

The Little Book of Puppets in Stories

This story has infinite variations that could keep you in stories for a whole year! The children's ideas will give you plenty of scope, and you could try some of the following:

* start the story with the wizard;
* start the story in the woods with the animals;
* start the story with a magic object (a small shiny stone, a little box, a perfume bottle filled with coloured water);
* make it a sensory story with pauses for things to see, smell, taste, touch, hear;
* use some simple sounds to accompany the story;
* let a child start the story off.

Or

* use a different puppet to start the story and bring in familiar characters from other stories;
* let the children tell a story with finger puppets to a big puppet;
* use the same puppets to explore feelings and personal situations. A dragon could be lonely, or a prince could be unkind. A dog could miss his mum, or a wizard could have some new glasses!

The Little Book of Puppets in Stories

Some stories to start you off with using puppets

We're Going on a Bear Hunt - Rosen & Oxenbury

The Very Hungry Caterpillar - Eric Carle

Dear Zoo - Rod Campbell (Campbell Books)

Whose Footprints? - Yabuuchi (Putnam)

Where the Wild Things Are - Maurice Sendak (Red Fox)

Mr Gumpy's Motor Car/Mr Gumpy's Outing - John Burningham (Red Fox)

Can't You Sleep, Little Bear? - Martin Waddell (Walker)

Tales of Wisdom & Wonder - Hugh Lupton (Barefoot Books)

South & North, East & West - The Oxfam Book of Children's Stories - Edited by Michael Rosen and Introduction by Whoopi Goldberg - Walker Books

When the World Began - Stories from Ethiopia - Edited by Elizabeth Laird - OUP

First Bible Stories - Retold by Margaret Mayo - Orchard Books

The Orchard Book of Stories From the Ballet - Retold by Geraldine McCaughrean - Orchard Books

Books for practitioners

Storylines - Ros Bayley (Lawrence Educational Publications)
ISBN: 1-903670-06-3
Puppets at Large - Linda Bentley (Positive Press)
ISBN: 1-904866-02-6
The Power of Puppets: Georgia Thorpe (Positive Press)
ISBN: 1-904866-03-4

Suppliers

Puppets by Post have hundreds of puppets of all shapes, sizes, types and characters. Find them at: www.puppetsbypost.com

For small musical instruments try:
WESCO Burnham Way Queen's Bridge Road Notts NG2 1NB
Tel: 0115 986 2126
sales@wescouk.co.uk

If you have found this book useful you might also like ...

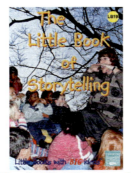

The Little Book of Storytelling
LB19
ISBN 1-904187-65-X

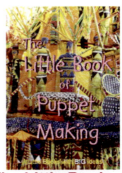

The Little Book of Puppet Making
LB23
ISBN 1-904187-73-0

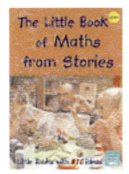

The Little Book of Maths from Stories
LB40
ISBN 1-905019-25-4

The Little Book of Language Fun
LB29
ISBN 1-904187-88-9

All available from

Featherstone Education   PO Box 6350
Lutterworth LE17 6ZA
T:0185 888 1212   F:0185 888 1360
on our web site
www.featherstone.uk.com
and from selected
book suppliers

The Little Books Club

Little Books meet the need for exciting and practical activities which are fun to do, address the Early Learning Goals and can be followed in most settings. As one user put it *" W h e n everything else falls apart I know I can reach for a Little Book and things will be fine!"*

We publish 10 Little Books a year – one every month except for August and December. **Little Books Club members receive each <u>new</u> Little Book on approval** and **at a reduced price** as soon as it's published.

Examine the book at your leisure. Keep it or return it. You decide.

That's all. No strings.   No joining fee.
No agreement to buy a set number of books during the year.
And you can leave at any time.

Little Books Club members receive -

- ♥ *each new Little Book on approval as soon as it's published*
- ♥ *a specially reduced price on that book and on any other Little Books they buy*
- ♥ *a regular, free newsletter dealing with club news and aspects of Early Years curriculum and practice*
- ♥ *free postage on anything ordered from our catalogue*
- ♥ *a discount voucher on joining which can be used to buy from our catalogue*
- ♥ *at least one other special offer every month*

There's always something in Little Books to inspire and help you!

Phone 0185 888 1212 for details